Ferns and Palms
for Interior Decoration

Ferns and Palms
for Interior Decoration

By JACK KRAMER

Drawings by Michael Valdez
(unless otherwise stated)

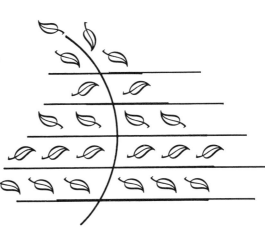

CHARLES SCRIBNER'S SONS
New York

Printed in the United States of America
Library of Congress Catalog Card Number 72-326

SBN 684-12930-2 (trade cloth)
SBN 684-12931-0 (trade paper, SL)

BOOKS BY JACK KRAMER IN THIS SERIES

Water Gardening
Miniature Plants Indoors and Out
Garden Planning for the Small Property
Hanging Gardens
Gardening with Stone and Sand
The Natural Way to Pest-Free Gardening
Ferns and Palms for Interior Decoration
(*Other titles in preparation*)

Contents

Introduction: Living Decoration

In the Victorian era, ferns were favorite plants; their graceful fronds were charming assets in any room. And I'm sure many readers will remember—some years later—the tall wicker stands with the ubiquitous Boston fern. Palms, too, through the years have had a place in the home, for they have a tropical look that few other plants have.

It is interesting to note that while ferns and palms handsomely complemented the ornate Victorian furnishings, they are equally at home in contemporary settings. They are the bit of nostalgia we all seek, or perhaps we have become better acquainted with their value as decorative house plants. In any case, these plants have withstood the test of time, a reliable guide rule whether for plant or product.

To be at their best, ferns and palms must be used intelligently in room decor for they are, in the main, large plants that require careful placement. Furthermore, unlike most house plants that require somewhat intensive care, ferns and palms, once established, almost take care of themselves. Most important, either plant will survive a shady corner.

If you think of all ferns as the Boston type you are in for a surprise. There are many other species and varieties, some bold in appearance and others delicate and lacy. The common names of holly fern, maidenhair fern, and sword fern give some indication of the versatility in the family. Palms offer a great variation in leaf and size. There are small palms and large ones; some are called butterfly palms, others fan palms, and so on. There is a wealth of plant material here for the home. (Also included in this book are the overlooked but beautiful Cycads or false palms.)

The point is that for room decoration, ferns and palms are superior to most house plants. They do not produce retarded small leaves after a few years like many philodendrons and dieffenbachias do, nor do they mysteriously lose leaves like rubber plants and fiddle-leaf figs. And with reasonable care, ferns and palms are relatively free of insects and disease. These are robust plants that will—even with minimum care—be with you for years to add charm and beauty to any area.

Jack Kramer

Ferns and Palms
for Interior Decoration

1. Ideal House Plants

If you ask a number of indoor gardeners what their favorite plants are, many will include ferns and palms in their answer. The same question asked of most interior designers or decorators brings the same answer: "Ferns and palms." And, finally, if you asked a horticulturist to name house plants that are decorative and easy to care for he will probably reply, "Ferns and palms."

If you want plants that will take care of themselves, provide graceful living accent in a room, tolerate neglect, palms and ferns are ideal. Of course, these plants are not the only ones for indoor decoration; there are others, but given equally adverse conditions, ferns or palms will outlive most house plants.

SIZE AND SHAPE OF PLANTS

The size of the plant not only affects its appearance but also its performance. Small plants will naturally be more difficult to grow than mature plants because, like children, the smaller ones require more time and patience. Mature plants, called specimen plants (in 10- to 20-inch pots), generally care for themselves once they are in a satisfactory place.

To many people, any plant with feathery or frondlike leaves is a fern but actually ferns differ widely in appearance. Some, like *Asplenium nidus*, are tall and vertical; others are low and bushy. Some, like the Boston fern varieties, gracefully cascade over their

Two stately Howea palms add grace and style to this handsome room; the one on the right appears like sculpture against a wall. (Max Eckert photo)

Ferns complement a living room; one a lush medium-size Boston fern at the right and the bird's-nest fern (*Asplenium nidus*) in left foreground. (Ken Molino photo)

containers; still others, such as Blechnums, have stiff fronds. There are infinite shapes, textures, and forms in ferns, and it is wise to study a plant carefully before you buy it. Specimen plants need something to stand on—a pedestal or a plant stand—and are not good in windows because the delicate fronds will be bruised from brushing against the glass. Many ferns depend on their exquisite symmetry (a rosette of lush green) for beauty; thus, one-sided plants are an eyesore. Of course, you can also grow large ferns in baskets

In a hanging basket *Polypodium aureum undulatum* is a special accent; it is perfect for the stairwell where it provides eye interest and drama. (Joyce R. Wilson photo)

Not a large plant, but dramatic in every aspect is *Rhapis excelsa*; it is a gentle note of elegance in this living room. (Photo by author)

suspended with wire or chain from ceilings. With their flowing fronds cascading over pot rims, ferns are a fountain of green unequaled by most plants.

Palms vary in shape and size but not as radically as ferns. Generally, palms are vertical, usually straight trunked, with crowns of fan-shaped or feather-shaped leaves. Palms are related to grasses, bamboos, and so forth, and have unique trunks that are hollow cylinder-like structures; in themselves the trunks can be most beautiful. Some are narrow ringed and glossy like bamboo, while others are massive and gnarled. Leaves range from small (the size of a human hand) to enormous, with fan-shaped fronds as in Rhapis and Livistona species, or the foliage may be feathery: Caryota, Howea to name a few.

This fine holly fern (*Crytomium*) is an attractive plant for table and desk; easy to grow. (Hort Pix photo)

Ferns and palms are very much part of this handsome living room. (Hedrich Blessing photo)

Look at plants from all sides, study the foliage, growth habit, form, and shape before you buy. Like room accessories, ferns and palms should be studied closely as to where they will show off most effectively in the home.

THE BEST FERNS AND PALMS

Like most plants, some varieties or species of ferns and palms are easier to grow than other kinds. They require a minimum of care, can tolerate untoward conditions if necessary, and are handsome. The

Boston fern *Nephrolepis exaltata* 'Bostoniensis' and its varieties have always been popular. These are attractive plants famed for their ease of culture in Victorian times when cool rooms were common. Varieties such as 'Whitmanii' and 'Rooseveltii' are stunning. Not as easy to grow indoors but still desirable are the lacy maidenhair ferns (Adiantums). They are smaller than Boston ferns but are more deli-

Asplenium bulbiferum (close-up of frond) (photo by author)

Asplenium viviparium

cate in appearance and require more attention, for overwatering or underwatering affects them deleteriously. Japanese holly ferns (Cyrtomium) are tough, able to withstand adverse conditions with ease, but the many species of stag's-horn ferns, on the other hand, are often difficult to grow indoors.

Adiantum tenerum

Some ferns for the beginner to try are:
Adiantum hispidulum (maidenhair fern)
Asplenium nidus (bird's-nest fern)
Cyrtomium falcatum (Japanese holly fern)
Lygodium scandens (Japanese climbing fern)
Nephrolepis exaltata 'Bostoniensis' (Boston fern)

Although there may be some dispute about the best ferns for indoors, two palms lead the way with almost universal acceptance. The bamboo palm (*Chamaedorea erumpens*) and the paradise palm (*Howea forsteriana* or *Kentia forsteriana*) are robust, handsome plants. They share all the desirable qualities of a good house plant: they can tolerate, in fact prefer, shady corners; need only enough water to keep soil moist; grow in summer and rest in winter. Perhaps not as graceful, but certainly a good plant, is the fishtail palm (*Caryota*). This overlooked gem is a veritable masterpiece in design and can be grown to perfection with little care.

Palms for the beginner to try are:

Caryota mitis (fishtail palm)
Chamaedorea erumpens (bamboo palm)
Howea forsteriana (Kentia palm or paradise palm)
Phoenix roebelinii (pigmy date palm)
Rhapis excelsa (lady palm)

NAMES AND NAMES

Because ferns are somewhat similar in appearance, and some palms resemble each other, it is a good idea to know the names of the plant so that there can be no confusion when you order by mail— Latin names are a universal means of identification. (Common names sometimes refer to many plants that look the same but are *not* the same.)

Latin names may seem confusing because of genus, species, and varieties, but actually they are simple to learn. A genus such as Nephrolepis is the same as a family name such as Jones; the species name such as *exaltata* is the same as a given name such as John, and a variety ('Whitmanii') is a particular kind of that species.

Botanical nomenclature changes occasionally, with one plant being put into another genus, among other technical changes. For the most part, here is the up-to-date classification of the most commonly cultivated ferns and palms:

FERNS
Adiantum capillus-veneris (southern maidenhair fern)
A. cuneatum (delta maidenhair fern)
A. hispidulum (maidenhair fern)

Cyrtomium falcatum

Aglaomorpha meyenianum (bear's-paw fern)
Asplenium bulbiferum (mother fern)
A. nidus (bird's-nest fern)
Blechnum occidentale (hammock fern)
Cibotium chamissoi (Hawaiian tree fern)
C. schiedei (Mexican tree fern)
Cyrtomium falcatum (Japanese holly fern)
Davallia pentaphylla (rabbit's-foot fern)

Humata tyermanni (bear's-foot fern)
Lygodium japonicum (Japanese climbing fern)
Nephrolepis exaltata 'Bostoniensis' (Boston fern)
Pellaea rotundifolia (button fern)
Platycerium vassei (stag's-horn fern)
Polypodium aureum (hare's-foot fern)
Pteris cretica (brake fern)
P. tremula (Australian brake)
Rumohra adiantiformis (leather fern)
Woodwardia orientalis (chain-fern)

PALMS

Areca (*Chrysalidocarpus*) *lutescens* (butterfly palm)
Caryota mitis (fishtail palm)
Chamaedorea elegans (*Neanthe bella*) (parlor palm)
C. erumpens (bamboo palm)
Chamaerops excelsa (windmill palm)
C. humilis (Mediterranean fan palm)
Howea belmoreana (*Kentia belmoreana*) (sentry palm)
H. forsteriana (*Kentia forsteriana*) (paradise palm, kentia palm)
Licuala spinosa (fan-shaped palm)
Livistona chinensis (Chinese fountain palm)
Phoenix canariensis (slender palm)
P. roebelinii (pigmy date palm)
Reinhardtia gracilis (window palm)
Rhapis excelsa (lady palm)
R. humilis (slender lady palm)
Syagrus weddeliana (*Cocos weddeliana*) (syagrus palm)

2. Selecting and Decorating with Ferns and Palms

Ferns and palms are part of the new nostalgia, and it is indeed good to see them becoming popular again. A well-grown specimen is a highly decorative plant that brings beauty and grace to any room. Ferns and palms are equally at home in living or dining room, bedroom or bath; in fact, one lush fern in any setting adds dimension to a room. In baskets hanging from ceilings they are a halo of green; on pedestals they are a spot of vibrant color, and a small plant on a coffee table adds charm to a setting. Palms, too, offer superb decoration, with their graceful wands of fronds. They are stately and elegant, and although tropical in appearance belong in almost any decor. Like chameleons they change with their surroundings and fit in a room, whether it is contemporary or period.

Because of their decorative value and their large size, most ferns and palms are expensive. A palm six feet high may cost $100, but like a piece of furniture it will become part of the room and be with you for years. Ferns, more modest in price, are about $15, although very large specimens may cost $50.

Select plants with care. Just don't buy anything; try to determine if the plant is in good health. Look for crisp green leaves, not wan foliage—healthy stems, not lax growth. Check the soil the plant is in: if it is caked you know you are buying a plant that has been on hand a long time and is apt to be not too robust.

As room accent, the lush Howea is stunning; it is graceful and fits the spot to perfection. (Hedrich Blessing photo)

The lacy pattern of a Chamaedorea palm stands in front of a doorway accenting a bronze sculpture. (Photo by author)

AS ROOM ACCENTS

Know where the plant you are buying will be used at home. Do you need a vertical accent to provide color and form against a bare wall, or is a low horizontal line along a window wall necessary? Ferns are broader and more massive than palms, and are bushy with rosette form. Palms are tall and horizontal; some are feathery and others are bold. The small ferns are best as table accents, while the larger ones are ideal for baskets. Because palms are mainly large plants they should be set on low pedestals and used as floor plants, although some of the smaller palms, like Livistonas, can be used for table ornaments.

A Boston fern on a handsome bamboo pedestal frames a doorway; this is a large plant in a 10-inch container. (Photo by author)

Some of the rabbit's-foot ferns (Davallias) are a study in sculpture, with their handsome, gnarled growth and fanciful foliage. Well-grown Boston ferns have striking rosettes of lush green, and the southern maidenhair fern (*Adiantum capillus-veneris*), with its wiry black branches and emerald green leaves, is a lacelike canopy of green. Use these smaller plants (6- to 8-inch pots) for spot accent on a table, desk, shelf, or bracket—they are never overpowering or obtrusive.

Palms excel as floor plants, but they should not be set directly on surfaces. Elevate them on a wooden platform or inverted clay pot (6 to 10 inches) to set them off beautifully. Used like sculpture in corners against white walls or to frame a fireplace, palms provide vertical accent. Remember that palms require a place of their own in a room.

Asplenium cristatum, a moderate-size fern, decorates this room corner; the attractive rattan plant stand sets it off perfectly. (McGuire Furniture photo)

ON PEDESTALS AND PLANT STANDS

Ferns are especially well suited to plant stands and pedestals; their rosette type of growth balances the vertical design of the stand. Some stands are made of wood or wrought iron, and the design varies. Pedestals are generally ornate, and vary from five to seven feet in height. Because pedestals are impressive pieces of furniture, the plants for them must be equally attractive so ferns are a fine choice. Furthermore, to be appreciated ferns must be seen from all sides, for their symmetry is their beauty. Crammed against a wall or a window they are not handsome, and since their delicate fronds are easily bruised, they soon turn brown and the plant becomes more of an eyesore than a delight.

Pedestals accommodate one plant; show it off to advantage. Any of the Boston fern varieties will be splendid attractions when elevated on pedestals. In the genus Polypodium there are several species of an essentially trailing nature. Davallias are charming too as pedestal plants and include *D. bullata,* the squirrel's-foot fern.

An overlooked but lovely fern is the large *Woodwardia orientalis,* with its blue-green broad pendant fronds; especially handsome on a pedestal, it is a stalwart performer and ideal for a cool, shady corner.

Good ferns for pedestals are:

Adiantum caudatum (trailing maidenhair fern)
Asplenium bulbiferum (mother fern)
Davallia bullata (squirrel's-foot fern)
Nephrolepis exaltata varieties (Boston ferns)
Polypodium aurem (hare's-foot fern)
Woodwardia orientalis (chain fern)

Palms are generally not suitable for pedestals because they are too vertical. Exceptions are *Caryota mitis* and young Syagrus palms (*Syagrus weddeliana*).

IN BASKETS

Plants in hanging containers placed at eye level have special appeal; many of the ferns mentioned for pedestal growing are ideal for baskets, too. Suspended from chains or rope in decorative containers, baskets of ferns put on a grand show and add dimension to

In a hanging basket this lacy fern hides the container; it is a fine decorative accent at eye level. (Photo by author)

a room. Indeed, they are so charming grown in this manner that many restaurants and public places use them for decoration.

The problem with plants in baskets has always been excess water dripping onto floors. Now, with the new drip-tray saucers and other devices, excess water will not stain floors. You can choose from clay clip-on saucers to plastic ones, or make your own water-catching devices with baking pans of sheet metal; make the pot and saucer into one unit so they appear esthetically pleasing. Nurseries have many wire and rope devices for hanging plants, and almost any container can serve as a basket for plants: a bucket, slatted wooden box, or wire basket.

Remember that hanging baskets filled with soil and plants are heavy and thus require strong supports. Hardware stores carry eye-bolts, screw eyes, brackets, and other ceiling hanging devices to hold the chain or rope that supports the container.

A slatted redwood basket is the container for the chain fern (*Woodwardia orientalis*). The basket is suspended with nylon filament. (Photo by author)

Potting basket plants is somewhat different from potting standard containers. Line slatted or wire containers with sphagnum moss, which comes shredded or in sheets, or with osmunda. Moisten the moss and place it firmly against the sides of the container. If soil sifting through the liner drops on the floor, set a layer of plastic or aluminum foil over the sphagnum or osmunda. Remember to punch small holes in the material so water can escape.

You can also set potted ferns in hanging containers (a pot within a pot); then cover the top with sphagnum moss. This method cuts down planting time and it is easy to refurbish the basket if necessary. However, it restricts plant growth. It is better to remove plants from their clay pots and set them directly in the soil. Then they do not dry out as rapidly as plants left in pots. Repotting basket plants depends on the size of the plant, but generally ferns only need to be repotted every two years. Frequent repotting results in poor growth since ferns do not like to be disturbed too often.

For additional information on ferns in basket containers, see *Hanging Gardens*, a companion volume in this series.

3. Keeping Ferns and Palms Beautiful

Ferns and palms can tolerate untoward conditions if necessary, but it is to your benefit to give them good care. Even with minimum attention the plants will prosper and be a pleasure to view, and there is always satisfaction in growing a plant to perfection.

Observation (along with care) is the key to healthy plants. Inspect ferns and palms frequently to see if the leaves are firm and of good luster; stems should be strong and flexible. If a plant does not grow well in one place, move it—a few inches one way or the other can make a difference. Drafts and heat pockets in rooms should be avoided.

FERNS

Most ferns revel in moisture and shade. A north or south location suits them fine, for there they are protected from the direct midday sun that can harm them, yet at the same time they receive all the light possible. Uniform temperature and humidity are beneficial, so watch thermometers to avoid fluctuating temperatures in the growing area. Most ferns thrive at 70° to 80° F during the day with a gradual decrease in temperature to 55° to 60° F at night.

Ventilation in the growing area should supply constant fresh air but no drafts; drafts are extremely injurious to plants. Because many ferns like coolness at the roots, it is a good idea to place pots on beds of gravel or cinders. This also supplies humidity through evaporation of excess water.

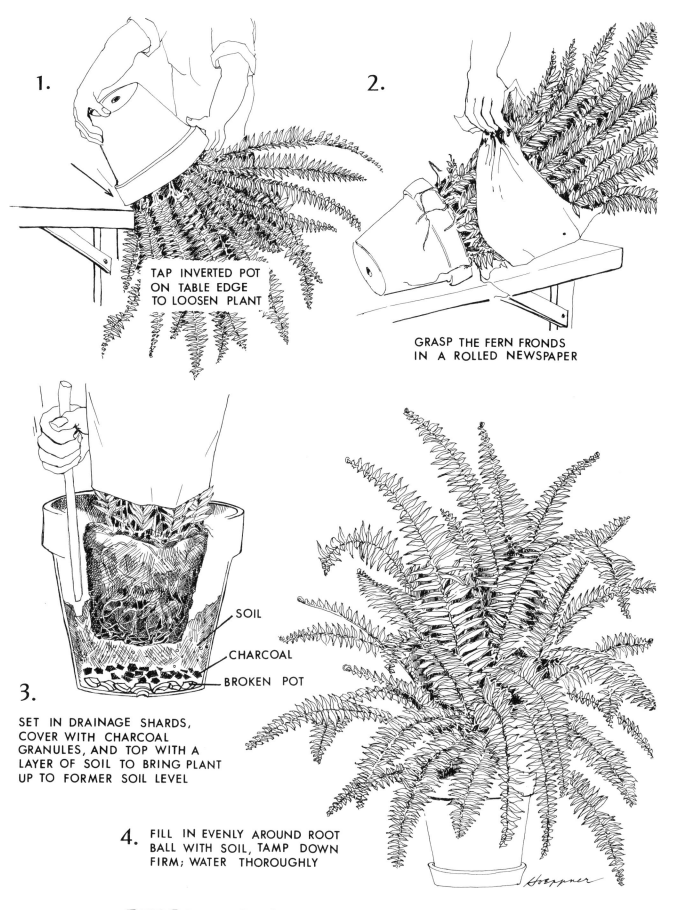

1. TAP INVERTED POT ON TABLE EDGE TO LOOSEN PLANT

2. GRASP THE FERN FRONDS IN A ROLLED NEWSPAPER

3. SET IN DRAINAGE SHARDS, COVER WITH CHARCOAL GRANULES, AND TOP WITH A LAYER OF SOIL TO BRING PLANT UP TO FORMER SOIL LEVEL

SOIL

CHARCOAL

BROKEN POT

4. FILL IN EVENLY AROUND ROOT BALL WITH SOIL, TAMP DOWN FIRM; WATER THOROUGHLY

REPOTTING A LARGE BOSTON FERN

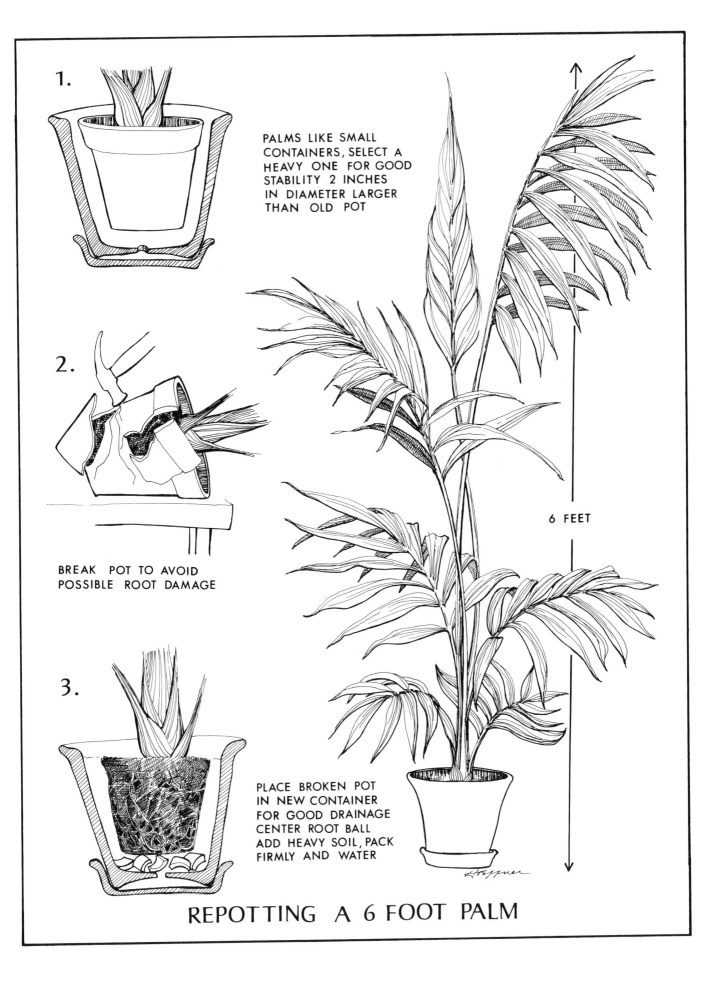

1. PALMS LIKE SMALL CONTAINERS, SELECT A HEAVY ONE FOR GOOD STABILITY 2 INCHES IN DIAMETER LARGER THAN OLD POT

2. BREAK POT TO AVOID POSSIBLE ROOT DAMAGE

3. PLACE BROKEN POT IN NEW CONTAINER FOR GOOD DRAINAGE CENTER ROOT BALL ADD HEAVY SOIL, PACK FIRMLY AND WATER

6 FEET

REPOTTING A 6 FOOT PALM

Asplenium nidus, the bird's-nest fern, is well grown; it receives diffused light here and hardly any sun. (Photo by Jack Barnich)

Select a porous potting soil so water may readily pass through it and a change of air in the soil is possible. A satisfactory soil consists of:

1 part leaf mold
1 part fibrous peat
1 part sand

Repot plants only when absolutely necessary; most like to be potbound, and a mature plant in a 12-inch pot can last 3 years without being disturbed. Smaller plants need more frequent repotting.

This lush specimen *Platycerium* grows on a chunk of tree bark anchored to the pillar; it is in a cool shady situation and thrives. (Photo by Jack Barnich)

Remember that with most ferns there is no cure once roots dry out and fronds droop. Watering dry roots does not perk up the foliage as it does with many other plants.

Avoid excessive feeding—most ferns react adversely to any feeding (for example, several plants I grow here develop brown leaves even with moderate feeding, but I do give weak solutions of fish emulsion, which seem very satisfactory).

I grow all my ferns in clay pots because clay allows moisture to evaporate gradually from within the walls, which is beneficial to ferns since they like their roots cool and moist. Plastic pots do not retain moisture within their walls and plastic is neither moist nor cool.

You can repot ferns at any time of the year, but the best months are February and March because warm weather, which encourages development and growth, is on the way. Use clean dry pots; soak new and old ones in water for a few hours. Unsoaked pots absorb a great quantity of water and rob the freshly potted plant of moisture. Try not to injure the roots of the plant when repotting it. Fern roots grasp the inside of the pot walls, so if you pull them loose they are injured. Try to tease the plant from its container after rapping it sharply against a table edge. If this doesn't work, you might have to break the container with a hammer. Because most clay pots are inexpensive and after a number of years unsightly, breaking the pot is not folly.

Once the plant is out of its container, crumble away old soil and trim dead roots (brown ones) slightly. If you are dealing with a large fern and don't want to bruise the plant unnecessarily, turn it upside down while it is in its pot and wrap the plant in a large towel or in newspaper. This protects the fronds and makes repotting easier. Place the plant in a new container on a generous bed of crushed gravel; add soil in and around the crown of the plant. Push down slightly (but not hard) to firm the soil. Do not jam the plant into the pot. Choose a pot that will be large enough for two years' growth but not so large that the plant will look ungainly. A plant from a 6-inch pot should go into an 8-inch container; one in a 10-inch container should go into a 12-inch pot, and so on.

Do not immediately put the fern in the growing area; water it thoroughly several times to make sure the soil is really soaked and all air pockets are eliminated. Place it in a bright place and water it moderately for a few weeks. Then put it in its permanent place in the room.

Watering ferns seems mysterious to most people because various conditions govern the watering schedule: pot size (large pots dry out slower than small ones), individual growing conditions, the weather, and the plant itself. In cloudy, cool weather plants grow slowly, if at all, and overwatering will not force them into growth—it will kill them. If your growing conditions lack humidity, too much water also

A *Rhapis* palm grows near a north window; the plant gets light but little sun and has grown into a healthy specimen. (Jack Barnich photo)

can cause the plant to die. Take into account all these variables when watering. Generally you can water large plants twice a week in spring and summer, once a week or every ten days in fall and winter when most ferns rest.

When you water, soak the plant and then allow it to dry out a bit before watering it again. Once a month place the plant in a tub of water for a few hours until air bubbles cease on the surface of the soil; this method leaches out salts that can accumulate and harm the plant. Do not use icy cold water for ferns because it will harm foliage; I leave a bucket of water standing overnight for use in the morning. Try not to get moisture on the fronds or a fungus may develop on the foliage. Keep tops of plants dry.

Remember to turn plants quarterly every month or so to ensure the beautiful symmetry of the fern (a lopsided plant isn't handsome, and it takes but a few minutes to turn the plant). Keep fronds from bruising by allowing enough space between plants or between plant and wall so fronds do not come in contact with anything.

PALMS

Most palms, especially the Howeas, will grow in almost any kind of soil—clay or sandy—but the majority need a well-balanced mix with proper drainage. We use 2 parts good loam topsoil, 1 part dried cow manure (available in packages), 1 part sand, and 1 part peat with a ½ cup of bone meal to a 10-inch pot.

Ferns may tolerate some stagnant water at the roots, but palms won't. They require a well-drained soil, so supply boxes and tubs with good drainage materials. Put in a 3-inch layer of coarse gravel or broken pot pieces (shards) in the bottom of the container. Then install a mound of soil and center the plant. If it is too low, add more soil; if it is too high, take out some soil. Fill in and around the collar of the plant with soil. Push down to eliminate air pockets in the mix, and firm the soil with your thumbs. Do not bury the crowns of the plant too deeply in the soil or rot may take place; on the other hand, be sure the crowns are not too high above the soil line or the plants will appear awkward in their containers.

The beauty of *Rhapis excelsa* is easily seen in this close-up photo. (Jack Barnich photo)

Provide adequate ventilation for palms; they like a good circulation of air. But once again be sure they are not in direct drafts that can injure them. Palms will tolerate temperatures from 45° to 85° F. indoors, but optimum growth takes place at 65° to 75° F. during the day, with a 15° nighttime drop in temperature.

Although ferns should not be allowed to dry out too much, palms can tolerate and seem to do better with a somewhat dry-to-the-touch soil, especially in winter when they rest. In spring and summer more liberal waterings can be applied: enough to flood the plant and drain into the saucer. Once a month try to leach out accumulated salts by dunking palms in a bucket of water for a few hours. Most palm fronds benefit if they are wiped with a damp cloth periodically or at least sprayed once a day with water in warm weather.

Palms grow slowly, so do not try to rush them into growth with additional feedings. In fact, fertilize palms only a few times in summer and not at all the rest of the year. Place plants where they will receive bright light; direct sun should be avoided.

4. Ferns and Palms for Special Places

Even though there are hundreds of house plants, few are decorative enough or suitable for a special place such as a garden room, patio, or terrace. Most house plants are too small, of awkward growth, or not symmetrically beautiful. But the fern, with its cascading fronds of green, is a miracle of nature's design, and palms, with their sculptural fronds, make dramatic silhouettes against sky or walls.

A large fern or palm in a garden room or enclosed pool immediately makes a statement and can thrive in the same container for several years without undue care. Because these rooms generally have large expanses of glass and are bright but not too sunny, ferns and palms are especially desirable, and they make a perfect foil for flowering plants.

On a patio or terrace palms heighten outdoor surroundings and serve as a link between the garden and paved area. Ferns make stellar basket subjects that frame a patio and add eye-level interest. Furthermore, they can be seen from all angles and the adjoining garden areas as well. Most plants have a tendency to grow one side toward the light, but ferns and palms always appear symmetrically handsome.

GARDEN ROOMS AND ENCLOSED POOLS

Lush ferns and stately palms are naturally handsome under glass; the picture is reminiscent of the lovely ferneries of the past. These plants are ideal choices, and once established they grow with little care. The initial investment may be costly, but it is far better to have a really permanent plant than to replace it frequently.

The closed atmosphere and high humidity of the garden room or pool especially favor ferns and palms, and generally any light bright position will suit them well. For these special places, which depend on drama to make them appealing, select really good specimens and put them in suitable containers so they will be with you for years.

Containers are available in many sizes and shapes. Clay pots, as mentioned, are best, but if you want an ornamental glazed pot or Chinese jardinière by all means have it. Slip the clay pot into the decorative container without repotting the plant. Because large containers are difficult to move, set them on dollies with casters.

When you buy your plant you will have no idea how long it has been in its original pot; you can, of course, grow it for a few years, but eventually you will have to repot it. Neither ferns nor palms like to be disturbed too often, so proceed with caution. See Chapter 3.

PATIOS AND TERRACES

In these areas you might want to use hanging baskets of ferns or a few tall palms as accents. Some species are more suitable for outdoor growing because of their size or growth habit than others; these are mentioned at the end of the chapter. In any case, when you select plants, base your decision on what they can do for the patio or terrace. Do you want leafy ferns or elegant palms? Do you want fine-textured foliage or plants with broad fronds? Each will have its own silhouette in the setting.

If you use ferns as floor plants or on low pedestals, group several together for a lush effect; one fern is rarely pleasing, but a group can be stunning. Seek the unusual palms: fishtail palms (Caryota) or the pigmy date palm *Phoenix roebelinii*. Small plants are not in scale with the large outdoors, so search for mature specimens.

In winter, protect outdoor plants from the weather. In most climates this means taking them in in early September and putting them outside in early April, although time varies throughout the country. When you are ready to move plants indoors, dollies are handy; otherwise you will need four or five people to move the plant.

Place a plant at a living room window to provide winter beauty, or, if there is no space, consider an unheated but not freezing room such as a garage or a spare porch. In cooler temperatures and sub-dued light, plants need much less water than normally. Keep the soil barely moist through winter months, when most palms and ferns are resting anyway. When warm weather starts put the plants out-side again to refresh them and resume regular watering.

FERNS FOR GARDEN ROOMS AND PATIOS

Adiantums. Group for a handsome display; these are effective either in corners or along walls, without interfering with traffic. The beauty of Adiantums is in their canopies of lacy green fronds. Set plants on low pedestals.

In this enclosed greenhouse-garden room, graceful ferns offer accent and color. (Max Eckert photo)

A large *Polypodium* fern is the feature of this garden room; behind it are palms.
(Max Eckert photo)

A small palm occupies a special place in a living room; used in this divider-planter it offers vertical accent without obstructing the view. (Ken Molino photo)

Blechnums. These stiff-leaved ferns provide a bold dramatic note in a room. Use mature plants. You will want only one as an accent because they are big and showy.

Cyrtomiums. These graceful Japanese holly ferns can do more for an area than most people realize. Capitalize on their cascading growth habit by placing them near but not against walls. Use an elevated base or pedestals for plants.

Even one large palm can provide the drama necessary for a garden room; here *Syagrus weddeliana* is the plant. (Hedrich Blessing photo)

The author's garden room has an assortment of ferns and palms. In the right corner is a Howea with a Boston fern in a basket above it. Hanging baskets contain *Woodwardia orientalis* and *Nephrolepis exaltata* 'Fluffy Ruffles.' In center foreground is *Chamaedorea elegans*. (Photo by author)

Davallias. The beauty of these ferns is in their lacy fronds and interesting gnarled, somewhat bizarre, but beautiful rhizomes. Grow Davallias as basket plants, anchored into sphagnum moss, for a splendid sight. Select varieties carefully; some are handsome, others are rangy.

Nephrolepis exaltata 'Bostoniensis' (Boston fern). This species includes many lovely varieties, and all are ideal for basket or pedestal growing. Some Boston ferns can grow to six feet in diameter, which is quite a spectacular sight in a high-ceilinged room.

A tree fern occupies a special place on the terrace; it is protected from direct sun. (Photo courtesy of California Association of Nurserymen)

Polypodiums. The single really outstanding species is *P. aureum undulatum*, with broad green fronds and pendant growth, which is always welcome in a special area. Because this plant can grow quite large, give it ample space.

Platyceriums. These are for an exotic touch; mainly grown on cork bark or slabs of wood, Platyceriums love moisture and humidity. *P. vassei* is well liked and *P. bifurcatum*, a shield of green.

Woodwardias. These popular chain ferns should be used more because the large specimens, with their broad, dark green and scalloped leaves, are a study in beautiful design. Grow these ferns on stands or in baskets for maximum beauty.

Woodwardia radicans is an excellent patio plant and will tolerate some sun. (Photo courtesy of California Association of Nurserymen)

PALMS FOR GARDEN ROOMS AND PATIOS

Caryotas. The tall specimens cannot be beaten for beauty; the sparse growth and sculptural patterns are outstanding against a bare wall.

Chamaedoreas. The bamboo palm *C. erumpens* has been recommended earlier in this book and is suggested again here because it is a stately plant, easy to grow, and highly decorative.

Howeas. The famous Howea palms, with their lovely graceful fronds, are at home in any area. Large plants are an umbrella of green.

Phoenix. There are several species that make good pot plants; *P. roebelinii* is perhaps the best known. These plants are not as graceful as some palms, but they are tough and can take abuse.

Rhapis. A favorite plant is *R. excelsa* and rightly so. It has attractive dark green wedge-shaped fronds, needs little care, and is always welcome indoors. Select bushy, strong plants.

This lovely stag's-horn fern (*Platycerium*) is like a painting on this patio wall providing drama and interest. (Hort Pix photo)

5. Ferns and Palms:
A Check List

The following lists of ferns and palms describe the plants I have grown through the years. Some are fifteen years old and were apartment denizens in Chicago (namely the bamboo palm *Chamaedorea erumpens* and the pigmy date palm *Phoenix roebelinii*). Others decorated my living room in Northfield, Illinois. In California for the last ten years I have had more than twenty-four assorted ferns and palms in tubs and boxes: some indoors, others for patio decoration.

When I added a garden room to my California house, many of the plants were given permanent places. None were ever grown in a greenhouse or with any special considerations. Recently, as space became available, I added many varieties of the Boston fern, namely 'Fluffy Ruffles,' 'Whitmannii,' and others as basket plants in the garden room, where the ceiling soars twenty feet and eye-level interest is needed.

Of all the ferns and palms I have grown, none gave undue trouble; they almost grew by themselves (except for a good supply of water). Some of my plants were presents from friends when they no longer had space for them; others were purchased through the years.

The following list does not include small or miniature ferns for dish gardens or fern cases; these are discussed in Chapter 8.

FERNS

ADIANTUM (MAIDENHAIR FERNS)
Their black shiny stalks and emerald-green leaves have given this group the name maidenhair ferns. The genus name Adiantum derives from *adiantos*, meaning dry, because most plants in this genus, even

Adiantum tenerum 'Wrightii'

Chamaedorea elegans (photo courtesy of Merry Gardens)

Polystichum aculeatum

Davallia fijiensis

Asplenium viviparium

after fronds have been wholly submerged in water, come out as dry as before. Not only are Adiantums amenable plants but they are also just the right size for indoors, never too big or too small. With their wands of graceful fronds the plants are desirable in almost any situation, but look best when used in groups, for then a lush and delicate feeling is achieved.

As a rule, Adiantums are easy to manage. They do not need sunlight; in fact, they will perish in direct rays because they prefer a dimly lit corner. As mentioned in Chaper 3, use porous soil with a good amount of decayed leaf mold, and do not pot the plants hard. Propagation is by spores or by divisions if the species have tufted crowns in early spring. (By the way, it will not harm the mature plant in any way if you cut fronds for flower decorations.)

A. capillus-veneris (southern maidenhair fern). Worldwide in distribution, this fern needs little encouragement to grow. It is robust, and the running rhizomes are easily distinguishable from all others since they have scales and are dark brown. In its natural habitat the plant will grow on a wall or rock or cling to almost any surface, so if it cascades over its pot let it be—you will have a healthier plant. Fronds are from 8 to 18 inches long, generally triangular or ovate in shape, thin and more or less transparent in texture. This useful species has many fine varieties: *A. c. v. crispulum*, and *A. c. v. undulatum* (unfortunately seldom seen).

A. caudatum (trailing maidenhair). This species is different from the majority of maidenhairs. The leaflets are pale dull green or grayish and the stalks are covered with short brown hairs that are more apparent as they approach the crown. This is a good basket plant that grows to 3 feet.

A. cuneatum (delta maidenhair). An old favorite, native to Brazil, and probably one of the most charming ferns you can grow. Fronds are 12 to 18 inches long, about 9 inches broad, and of more or less upright habit. The plant produces an immense quantity of fronds from a tufted crown all year if soil is kept moist. It is readily propagated from spores that root in any soil when they fall from the plant. Many varieties have been cultivated, with *A. c. gracillimum* still occasionally seen.

Asplenium viviparum

A. hispidulum (maidenhair fern). This native of Australia and New Zealand has slender but stiff hairy stalks 8 to 15 inches long. The fronds are dark green color when mature, metallic when young. The maidenhair fern is easily grown and likes moist soil.

A. tenerum (brittle maidenhair). This is a big, impressive plant; fronds are covered with brown hairs and produced from a creeping underground rhizome. The fronds have an elegant character and can grow up to 4 feet; because of their glossy green color they contrast beautifully with the black stalks. A truly handsome interior plant that is always a show.

ASPLENIUM (SPLEENWORT FERNS)

These ferns are enjoying a renaissance and rightly so: some are quite handsome, and useful indoors. The common name evolved because once these plants were used to cure afflictions of the spleen. These ferns differ from other ferns because the spore masses attached to the veins are oblique to the midrib and are of a peculiar oblong shape. The stalks of most species are black and succulent. Mature plants are impressive, and those with cascading fronds make handsome basket subjects.

Plants are generally easy to grow, but they do require almost perfect drainage as excess water standing in plant saucers will eventually cause foliage to become flabby. Aspleniums dislike hard potting and prefer a loose open soil. They will tolerate more sun than most ferns, but they are really at their best in shade: they are then shiny green. Amazingly free of insects, the Aspleniums are a highly decorative group.

A. bulbiferum (mother fern). This favorite from New Zealand and Australia is popular because it grows rapidly and tolerates a dry atmosphere. The fronds are 24 inches long and about 10 inches broad. The plant has a rather upright habit, although the fronds are usually pendulous, covered with young plants at certain times of the year.

A. nidus (bird's-nest fern). A unique species with much larger fronds than most ferns, sometimes 6 feet long and 12 inches wide. They are elliptical and spear shaped. The fronds, instead of growing horizontally at first, are arranged upright in a rosette around the succulent

Asplenium bulbiferum

crown, thus leaving the hollow center funnel shaped. The plants need more heat than most ferns and will thrive in merely bright light, i.e., no sun. Inspect frequently for slugs or snails; they adore the succulent growth of *A. nidus.*

A. viviparum. A handsome fern with dark green fronds 12 to 24 inches long and 8 inches broad which are borne on firm greenish stalks about 9 inches high. The leaflets are closely placed and dense, and the plant has a feathery appearance. This plant prefers a sandy growing mix with only a little soil.

BLECHNUM

This is a small genus of plants from tropical and south temperate regions. Several have distinct ornamental value because of their graceful leathery fronds of light or dark green.

If you have had trouble growing other kinds of ferns, try Blechnums, for they are facile and rewarding plants. They can grow in almost any soil and need only a well-ventilated, light place. Young plants are not as handsome as the well-grown mature ones which are excellent for interior decoration.

B. brasiliense. A popular fern from Brazil and Peru; it is strong growing and very decorative. The stem, with dark brown scales, grows to 36 inches and is densely clothed at the crown. Fronds are oblong and spear shaped to 40 inches long and about 12 inches wide. Leaves are leathery and of a lovely green color.

B. occidentale (hammock fern). A rather dwarfish fern, with 9- to 15-inch long fronds about 4 inches across. Stalks are flexible and of a leathery texture; leaflets are heart shaped. *B. occidentale* makes a dense plant.

B. moorei. Somewhat more graceful than other Blechnums, with its wide, bright green, leathery leaflets, this fern is easy to grow and makes a fine table accent.

B. spicant (deer fern). A native of northern California and the Northwest which produces two types of fronds: the sterile fronds are narrow, dark glossy green, and spreading or angled; the fertile fronds are erect and very narrow. Give this specimen deep shade, moisture, and a woodsy soil.

CIBOTIUM (TREE FERNS)

Similar to outdoor Dicksonias, Cibotiums are quite easy to grow and provide exceptional elegance in any area. The fronds are delicate traceries of pale green, graceful and arching, and can grow quite tall. Plants require a shady place and will thrive in coolness or warm temperatures.

Tree-fern stock is available from mail-order dealers and looks like a piece of a tree trunk, with one or two lumps covered with a reddish-brown silky down. Don't panic if you think you have spent your money for nothing; once a tree fern is planted, growth is almost certain to start. Put the bottom third of the tree piece into a friable soil, and keep it damp, *never* soggy. *Do not bury the entire trunk*—just keep enough soil around the bottom to encourage growth. Fronds continue to grow at the rate of one a month as long as the plant receives plenty of moisture. Each frond lasts a few months. When a frond turns yellow, cut it from the plant close to the trunk. Spray or sponge the fronds with a cloth dampened with warm water to keep the foliage handsome.

C. chamissoi. A handsome robust fern with spear-shaped leaflets that grow to 20 inches long and are deeply serrated and toothed, carried on long, slender, and downy brown stalks.

C. menziesii. This fern has a short, stout, fibrous trunk and delicate glossy green serrated leaflets. Fronds are triangular in shape.

C. schiedei. One of the most handsome ferns you can find, native to Mexico and Guatemala. Fronds are elegantly cascading, triangular in shape, and can grow 10 feet in length. They are three-times divided and borne on stout brownish trunks from crowns covered with dense brown hairs. The spear-shaped leaflets come to a narrow point. A very lacy and ornamental plant.

CYRTOMIUM (HOLLY FERNS)

A fine group of ferns that look more like holly. The stems are densely clothed with broad leaflets, and plants are tough enough to withstand city apartment conditions.

These plants like a loose woodsy soil and require excellent drainage. Give them coolness and a shady corner. Keep soil evenly moist.

Cyrtomium falcatum

C. falcatum (holly fern). Most common in the genus. The holly fern has handsome, dark green foliage and graceful manner of growth and makes an excellent house plant.

C. f. rochefordianum. A cultivar of the above species. It has dense green leaflets and is a robust grower. A favorite plant because of its scalloped foliage of high luster—grows easily, too.

DAVALLIA (RABBIT'S-FOOT FERNS)

These are epiphytic ferns, that is, they are mainly air plants and do well on pieces of cork bark or in hanging baskets. Davallias are characterized by long, exposed, and climbing hairy rhizomes that are bizarre but beautiful. At times these ferns have been called rabbit's-foot, hare's-foot, and squirrel's-foot ferns since the rhizomes resemble the anatomy of those animals.

Davallias should be elevated above the rim of the pot, never buried in the soil. The plants do badly in heavy soils; they require a compost of light materials such as osmunda or sphagnum, with some good leaf mold. They require more water than most ferns, and indeed appreciate a humid atmosphere during the growing season, but in winter they must be carried somewhat dry (but never so dry that the rhizomes shrivel). Give Davallias good light (they will even take some sun), and if you have a mature plant and need greens for cutting, it doesn't harm the plant to cut a few fronds (which, by the way, last a long time in water) for decorative arrangements.

D. bullata (squirrel's-foot fern). From Japan and Java, this really elegant scandent fern is of medium growth. The creeping rhizomes (stems) are clothed with reddish brown scales that resemble a squirrel's paw. The fronds are densely covered with 8- to 12-inch long and 4- to 8-inch broad triangular foliage, and are leathery and bright green. This is an extremely handsome room plant.

D. canariensis. This fern is smaller than *D. bullata* and more delicate in appearance, with 12-inch fronds (sometimes 12 inches broad) that are light green and leathery in texture. The stems or rhizomes are stout and creeping and curve over the pot sides.

D. fijiensis plumosa. A charming fern from the Fiji Islands. It has thick rhizomes and handsome, finely cut fronds that are borne on upright strong stalks and are 6 to 9 inches long and 12 inches broad. Fronds make a deltoid outline and are brilliant green; they are somewhat pendant when mature. A really elegant fern that requires a sandy soil.

D. heterophylla. An unusual Davallia whose entire fronds are 2 to 6 inches long and of a leathery texture. This fern, with a creeping scaly rhizome, needs a shallow pot.

D. mariesii. Similar to *D. bullata* but smaller, with elongated triangular fronds and gray rhizomes. Foliage is 8 to 12 inches long and 4 inches broad. A nice small plant that provides a lovely green accent.

D. pentaphylla. A dwarf-growing fern from Java and the Polynesian Islands. Fronds are produced from a scaly rhizome. Foliage is metallic green when young, dark green when mature.

D. solida. Of medium growth, this Davallia has harsh leathery fronds about 24 inches long and 12 inches broad. Fronds are borne on strong upright stalks about 6 inches tall.

Lygodium (Climbing Ferns)

A small genus, the name Lygodium derives from *lygodes*, meaning flexible. These are climbing or twisting ferns. The fronds of Lygodiums are different from most ferns because they are of stalklike growth and can grow to 20 feet. The leaflets are connected to the stalk by primary and secondary petioles. Plants require a well-drained, somewhat acid soil and revel in winter sun and dappled summer sunlight. Keep soil moist at all times.

L. japonicum. This very pretty fern is a real climber of slender growth and somewhat bushy habit. It is a native of Japan and China and takes well to indoor culture. The fronds are finely cut, brilliant green, and can grow to 10 feet. This plant requires good light and is at its best in a hanging container; a mature plant is a real display.

L. palmatum (Hartford fern). This is a delicate-looking plant with pale green stalks and palmate leaves. Of special merit, it makes a bold appearance.

Davallia canariensis

NEPHROLEPIS (SWORD FERNS)

Nephrolepis is the sire of the long chain of Boston fern varieties. The plants have medium green fronds growing to 48 inches, generally pendant and flowing. The Boston fern was a single variant of this fern, and from it has come a long line of varieties, one prettier than the other. The plants retain the luxuriant flowing green leaves and make superior house plants.

The history of the Boston fern is interesting and started with the Florida species *N. exaltata*. This fern, when introduced into commerce, did exceptionally well, growing to huge dimensions. It easily produced plantlets from scaly runners and in a short time became a favorite house plant.

The plants remained popular until about 1900 when a shipment from a Philadelphia grower to a Boston distributor showed it to be different from the true *N. exaltata*. It was considered another species, but this error was discovered in short order, and in 1896 the new plant was officially named *N. e.* 'Bostoniensis.' Today the original cultivar 'Bostoniensis' has largely been replaced by recent varieties.

The Boston varieties require copious watering in spring and summer, prefer large pots, and do not like to be disturbed. They can grow to great dimensions. The plants grow quickly and like a rich soil; they quickly deplete the soil of nutrients and require some additional light feeding during growing season. Winter sunlight is fine, but during the rest of the year the Boston varieties need a bright but not sunny spot.

N. exaltata. This is the sword fern hardly ever seen in cultivation. The plant has yellow-green to medium green fronds ranging from 24 to 80 inches long, with pendant and leafy growth.

N. e. 'Childsii.' A dwarf, slow-growing, waxy green choice plant.

N. e. 'Fluffy Ruffles.' An absolute beauty with heavily ruffled fronds and lush growth.

N. e. 'Norwoodii.' Has lacelike fronds up to 18 inches long; fresh, green, and dense growth.

N. e. 'Rooseveltii.' Another ruffled beauty of robust growth; similar to sword fern.

Pellaea rotundifolia

Nephrolepis exaltata 'Bostoniense'

N. e. 'Verona.' A popular Boston fern with lacy pendulous fronds.

N. e. 'Whitmannii.' With its dense, thickly clothed fronds, this is an elegant plant.

PLATYCERIUM (STAG'S-HORN FERNS)

The name of this group of plants derives from *platys* (broad) and *keras* (horn) because the fertile fronds of Platyceriums resemble stag's horns. This is a small genus of plants from the Philippines and temperate Australia. You have no doubt noticed Platyceriums because they are unique, easily recognizable by the broad forked fronds.

The plants are essentially for places where water stain on floors is no problem, since most Platyceriums grow best on slabs or cork bark rather than in pots. Anchor osmunda or sphagnum to the wood and attach the plant to it with wire. These air plants do not want their roots smothered in soil; the two I grew in soil never did amount to much. Plants require a bright location, plenty of water, and high temperatures of at least 65°F at night and 80°F by day. For garden rooms and solariums Platyceriums are fine, but for indoor decoration—living or dining room—they are rarely acceptable because of difficulty in watering them.

P. alcicorne (*bifurcatum*) (common stag's-horn fern). The most popular species, this fern grows on tree branches in Australia, Java, the East Indies, and Madagascar. Unlike most species, it will succeed at somewhat cool temperatures. The barren fronds are rounded and convex with wavy edges and downy when young. Fertile fronds grow to 36 inches, are clustered and somewhat upright in habit, are forked, and have a leathery texture. Variety *majus* is more robust, greener. By far the best in the group.

P. 'Bloomii.' A Florida cultivar, with rounded basal leaves and broad and forked fertile fronds that are upright at first but cascade as the plant matures.

P. grande. A magnificent fern. The barren fronds are large, stalkless, and nearly rounded. The upper portion is divided into a number of broad blunt segments, pale green in color. The fertile fronds may be 60 inches long, cascading, and are usually produced in pairs.

P. hillii. This fern has a fresh green color with rounded basal leaves; fertile fronds are erect, fan shaped, and divided at the lobes.

Rhapis excelsa

Platycerium vassei

Polypodium (Polypody Ferns)

This large genus of ferns includes some attractive members that make ideal room decoration. Mainly from Central and South America, the plants have fronds that are large, arching, and graceful but not as delicate in appearance as other ferns. For this reason Polypodiums are often overlooked, and yet as house plants they are superior because they are easy to grow.

Plants do best in shallow baskets of humus and sand kept uniformly moist all year, except in the winter months when they can be carried barely moist. Provide winter sun for Polypodiums, for without it they die. In summer, however, provide shade. There are only a few cultivated species, and these are mainly basket plants because of their pendant growth.

P. aureum (hare's-foot fern). A popular strong-growing species with bold habit and massive foliage sometimes 5 feet long and 2 feet wide. The rhizomes are knobby, somewhat scaled, and of a shining bright brown color, which lends the plant its other name: golden polypody. There are several varieties of this plant; all are fine decorative subjects.

P. polycarpon. A small-growing species with broadly triangular fronds; generally an upright grower of rather nice appearance.

P. subauriculatum (jointed polypody). A decorative basket fern with graceful fronds borne on heavy rhizomes. It is slow growing but desirable.

Pteris (Brake Ferns)

The Greek name *Pteris* was probably derived from the word feather, an illusion to the shape of the fronds. The group as a whole offers a wide variety of plants, but few are large enough to be dramatic, although several of the smaller species are charming. Because there are so many kinds of brakes, nomenclature is somewhat confused, and often plants are sold under incorrect names.

Even with their shortcomings, brake ferns are desirable for the novice gardener because they grow so easily. Most Pteris varieties can tolerate almost any kind of soil and will sustain themselves in the most subdued light.

Polypodium vulgare undulatum

P. cretica. This is an unusual plant with somewhat feathery growth and many variants. The typical species comes from the Himalayas and has 6- to 12-inch fronds that are borne on erect wiry stalks. The leaves are somewhat leathery and have a papery texture. You will find varieties with crested, sword-shaped, and fan-shaped leaves.

P. dentata. A dense fern with broad fronds to 24 inches long; fronds have a fresh green color and are finely serrated.

P. ensiformis (sword brake). A small fern with fronds about 10 inches long with long terminal leaflets.

P. e. 'Victoriae.' Much prettier than the species, this fern is slender and graceful, with either short, bushy, and sterile leaves or tall, slender, and fertile leaves. The sterile leaves have sharply serrated edges and are marked with silver bands and edged in green. Give the plant coolness.

P. quadriaurita (silver brake). This plant has somewhat leathery fronds to 36 inches long.

P. q. argyraea. A very handsome variety of the above species. Leaflets end in tail-like points banded in white; leaves are bright green. The plant can grow very large and needs winter sunlight. Keep soil moist.

P. tremula (Australian brake). A strong-growing plant. Its fronds, with their soft green color and paperlike texture, can grow to 36 inches, which make quite a display. Plant grows fast in winter sun and shade in summer. Likes good humidity.

RUMOHRA

A little-known genus, with one species occasionally offered by suppliers:

R. adiantiformis. Called the leatherleaf fern, this plant has creeping and ascending rhizomes; leaves are broad and closely spaced, dark green and leathery in appearance. It can grow to 12 inches. Plants require excellent drainage and a shady place at the window.

WOODWARDIA (CHAIN FERNS)

A small genus with some interesting ferns, Woodwardias are

tough and amenable plants. Fronds are graceful and become pendant with age.

Plants can be easily grown under cool conditions (45° to 55°F) and with bright light but little sun. Give them ample moisture most of the year, although they can be carried somewhat dry in winter. Repot infrequently because, like most ferns, Woodwardias resent being disturbed. There are now two species available at nurseries:

W. orientalis. A highly decorative fern with leathery fronds that are of a deep crimson color when young. The spear-shaped leaflets, which sometimes grow to more than 1 foot, are wavy and deeply cleft.

W. radicans. A handsome and strong-growing fern; leaflets are 12 to 16 inches long, spear shaped, leathery, and of a brighter green than *W. orientalis.*

PALMS

ARECA (CHRYSALIDOCARPUS) (BUTTERFLY PALMS)

A group of feathery palms from Madagascar with one species that is an outstanding house plant. Plants need a rich soil and plenty of water all year, except in winter when they can be grown somewhat dry.

C. lutescens (butterfly palm). A most beautiful plant with green and golden stems ringed in the fashion of bamboo. The feathery fronds are light green and elegantly arched. The leaflets are twisted, making handsome patterns. Before the discovery of Howeas, *C. lutescens* was *the popular indoor palm,* but it is hardly seen today.

CARYOTA (FISHTAIL PALMS)

Here is an overlooked genus of wonderful plants native to Asia, Malaysia, and Australia. The foliage, on long arching petioles, is wedge shaped, like a fish's tail. Young plants are apt to be straggly, but mature specimens are handsome, with a central trunk and arching fronds.

The plants tolerate sun but prefer a bright, somewhat shaded location. Fishtail palms seem to thrive in any soil that is kept evenly moist, and they are rarely attacked by insects or disease. Repot only when necessary, and trim the leaves, which have a tendency to be-

Caryota species (unidentified)

Chamaedorea elegans

come brown and brittle at the edges. Mature plants are difficult to find but worth the search.

C. mitis. The most popular fishtail palm. It grows to about 9 feet, and has dark green, leathery, wedge-shaped fronds.

C. urens (wine palm). This plant has branching stems that carry huge leaflets. Although the wine palm has sparse fronds it is still handsome indoors.

CHAMAEDOREA

A genus of remarkable palms from the humid rain forests of Mexico and Central and South America. Shade-loving plants with either single or multiple trunks, most Chamaedoreas make premium house plants for they can live in shade.

With vertical growth, plants are carefree and in large pots can live for a dozen years as long as soil is top-dressed occasionally. Although Chamaedoreas are easy to grow, they do have one requirement: leaves must be wiped frequently with a damp cloth to keep them in good health.

C. elegans (*Neanthe bella*) (parlor palm). Known under several common names, this is a wonderful, dense-foliaged palm. It has pinnate leaves arching from graceful stems on plants that rarely exceed 36 inches; needs shade.

C. erumpens (bamboo palm). Here is just about the best house plant you can buy. It has upright stalks of bamboolike stems and lovely arching fronds. The bamboo palm, which can grow to 8 feet indoors, prefers shade.

C. graminifolia. A very delicate graceful palm with light green slender leaflets spaced farther apart than most Chamaedorea species.

C. tenella. An unusual charming dwarf broad-leaved palm; it is an upright grower to 30 inches; unique in the genus. An excellent plant.

CHAMAEROPS

In Greek, *Chamaerops* means dwarf. The genus is represented by one or two species of varying growth but of dwarf stature. A general characteristic of the plants is the branching of the trunks at the base, with stiff fan-shaped leaves in almost a circular pattern. Leaves are deeply cut, usually dark green, but plants are quite variable and exceptions occur. The leaf stalk is spiny and may vary from a few inches to a few feet in length.

Plants can take sun if necessary and require good quantities of water in summer, but not as much the rest of the year.

C. excelsa (windmill palm). Technically known as *Trachycarpus fortunei*, this palm has a solitary hairy trunk with fan-shaped, some-folded dark green leaves. An especially attractive sculptural plant worth the search.

C. humilis (Mediterranean fan palm). This species appears in many forms and sizes and may be a small bushy plant to 3 feet or much taller with open growth. The color of leaves ranges from light to dark green to dark gray and glaucous green. Some plants have a woolly down on young foliage, which disappears with age.

HOWEA (KENTIA) (SENTRY PALMS, PARADISE PALMS)

These palms have a narrow natural habitat and are native only to the Lord Howe Islands in the Pacific. Also grown under the genus name Kentia they are variously called sentry palm, Howea palm, thatch palm, and so forth. Under any name they are tough plants that tolerate untenable conditions and still look handsome.

Naturally upright, Howeas, once established, can grow to 10 feet indoors, with lovely dark green arching fronds. They are indeed one of the finest plants for indoor decoration, but for all their use they are not as easy to grow as some other palms.

Howeas must have a good rich soil, plenty of water, and a place where there is some dappled sunshine. In their seedling stage they require great care, but once established they need only routine house plant care. Repot them only when absolutely necessary; they hate to be disturbed, and repotting will set them back years.

H. belmoreana (sentry palm). This is a slow-growing tree, compact in habit, with curving dark green leaves.

H. forsteriana (paradise palm). Grows faster than the type above. The paradise palm has dark green feathery leaves that grow to 10 feet and form an open crown. This is a stellar house plant.

LICUALA

These small palms, originally from Asia and the Pacific Islands and Australia, have a solitary or clustered stem. Rarely seen, Licualas are good tub palms. Their leaves grow in a circular pattern and are pleated like a fan.

Plants require little care; give them a porous soil and a shady place. Only these few species are in cultivation.

L. grandis. The trunk is solitary and grows to about 6 feet, with erect stems carrying bright green leaves in a circular pattern. The petioles are slender and toothed.

L. spinoso. Denser and fuller than *L. grandis*, this palm has clusters of glossy green leaves parted in the center into pleated segments. Rigid petioles covered with thorns.

LIVISTONA (FOUNTAIN PALMS)

Native to Eastern Asia, Malaya, the Philippines, New Guinea, and Australia, this group of palms is frequently called fountain palms. Livistonas are exceedingly handsome plants, with dense crowns of leaves on long spiny petioles. They make handsome indoor plants, although they are slow growing.

Like most palms, Livistonas need a shady place with a somewhat moist soil kept slightly dry in the winter. They prefer coolness and strongly resist insects or disease. Fountain palms make an absolutely stunning room accent against a white wall.

L. chinensis (Chinese fountain palm). This is the most popular palm in the genus, with fine fan-shaped crowns of leaves on arching stems.

PHOENIX (DATE PALMS)

A genus indigenous to Africa and Asia that includes the pigmy date palm *P. roebelinii*, it is tough to find a better indoor tree to grow. It will stay in the same pot for many years, needs little attention, and thrives in the darkest corner if it has to.

The plant needs lots of water most of the year, with less moisture in the winter months; then the soil should be somewhat dry. If you have a place indoors where no other plant prospers, by all means try the date palm; it is almost indestructible.

P. canariensis. A stately palm somewhat denser than *P. roebelinii*; it has arching glossy green leaflets. Needs some training to be attractive.

P. dactylifera. This is the popular date palm. It is not an especially good house plant, but young plants are seen occasionally and can be used indoors. Has needlelike leaves; thorny at base.

P. roebelinii (P. loureiri). Grows to 8 feet eventually, but it may take 15 years. Generally about 5 feet tall, with plumelike fronds borne from a brown hairy trunk.

Reinhardtia (Window Palms)

A genus of dwarf palms from Central America. Although seldom seen, they do make excellent indoor plants and are unusual and always beautiful. One species is available:

R. gracilis. Its leaves are borne on long slender stalks with waxy green bilobed foliage. Spaces between the ribbed leaves give the plant its name of window palm. Leaf ends are beautifully scalloped. The plant can grow to 6 feet indoors. It needs ample moisture and a well-drained soil, and prefers a north exposure.

Rhapis (Lady Palms)

Called lady palms, this genus of small but graceful plants is somewhat bushy and superficially resembles bamboo. The reedlike trunks are handsome, and the foliage is dark green. Native to eastern parts of Asia, Rhapis species make ideal pot plants, with a graceful habit of growth seldom matched by most plants.

Keep plants in shade; in sun they tend to become yellow. They like a rich soil kept moist but never wet; wipe leaves with a damp cloth to keep them in good health.

R. excelsa (lady palm). Stems of this palm are about 1-inch thick and rigid, with 5 to 8 stiff leaflets in palmate formation. A mature plant is a study in light and shadow and especially pleasing as a room accent.

R. humilis (slender lady palm). Taller than *R. excelsa* and not as graceful. Leaves form semicircular fans with 10 to 20 leaf segments that are deeply cut like fingers.

Phoenix canariensis

SYAGRUS (SYAGRUS OR COCO PALMS)

Decorative feather-leaved palms native to Brazil, now seen in many public buildings for lobby decoration. Plants have a light delicate look and can take a great deal of neglect if necessary. Ideally they prefer a shady spot and an evenly moist soil.

S. weddeliana (Cocos weddeliana). With a central trunk topped with a crown of yellow-green fronds, this palm needs little attention and grows well with minimum care.

6. Plants That Resemble Ferns and Palms

Many plants that are not really ferns or palms are frequently referred to as members of these families. If plants such as Dracaenas have a growth habit similar to a palm, they are often called a palm, but Dracaenas are actually members of the lily family. Yuccas, with their clumps of sword-shaped leaves, are occasionally called palms, as are Aloes and Cordylines because they have a remote resemblance to palmlike leaves or habit of growth. Beaucarnea is yet another lily sometimes masquerading as a palm. And *Dizygotheca elegantissima*, a fine house plant, with handsome, dark green leaves in a circular pattern that resemble an umbrella, is also, at times referred to as a palm.

Asparagus sprengeri, a favorite indoor plant, with graceful wands of feathery foilage, is often called a fern (and it certainly looks like one) and yet it belongs to the lily family. Selaginellas, fern-allies, seen in terrariums, are actually members of the Selaginellaceae but resemble their cousins. *Begonia foliosa* is called the fern begonia, another popular indoor subject.

Cycads, an ancient family of plants, can even confuse an expert gardener because they combine the graceful fronds of palms and the delicate tracery of ferns. Little known, these overlooked plants are superb for indoor growing.

We are including these groups of plants although they are not true ferns or palms because they are so useful indoors, make elegant plants, and adapt extremely well to indoor growing.

FERNLIKE PLANTS

Asparagus sprengeri. A favorite house plant and a spectacle of delicate green tracery when it is mature. Plants are bushy, and as they get older fronds become pendant and overflow from the pot.

A. plumosa, with plumes of a delicate feathery green, is an upright grower. It is also called a fern, although it is a member of the lily family.

Begonia foliosa (fern begonia). This plant has tiny dark green leaves on pendant stems. It is charming and from a distance certainly looks like a fern.

Begonia foliosa is known as the fern begonia because of its tiny leaves and pendent habit. (Joyce R. Wilson photo)

Selaginella. In this group are many handsome plants overlooked until recently as decorative basket plants. There are several species, but perhaps *S. emmeliana* is the most commonly seen. It has fronds of light green, triangular leaflets that are dense and lovely. *S. pulcherrima* is another study in beautiful tracery, and *S. versicolor* is a bushy beauty. These plants thrive best in a bright and very moist condition. I found specimen-sized Selaginellas at Woolworth's last year, and they have proved to be fine for indoor growing.

PALMLIKE PLANTS

Beaucarnea recurvata. A plant with a bulbous base and ribbonlike leaves. It requires a sunny place and an evenly moist soil.

Cordyline. There are several species with crowns of broad, exquisitely colored leaves. They make excellent tub plants. Large specimens have arching stems and a unique habit or growth. Desirable in any area.

Dracaena marginata. Called the "decorator plant," this sculptural beauty is hard to beat in a living room. Branched curved trunks are topped with crowns of arrow-shaped dark green leaflets edged in red. Plants are indeed handsome and require little light; keep soil on the dry side.

Pandanus vietchii. A splendid variegated-foliage plant with toothed-leaved edges growing in a wide rosette. Sometimes called the screw pine, large specimens of this plant are ideal decorator plants and live for years with little attention. Put them in a somewhat shady place and keep soil evenly moist.

Yuccas. This family of plants offers much indoor beauty; Yuccas are superior accents. In ornamental tubs they are unique and virtually impossible to kill. Give Yuccas a somewhat sunny place and keep soil on the dry side. I have grown *Y. aloifolia tricolor* and *Y. a. marginata* for years; they are in 8-inch pots and make excellent floor plants. Give them ample space though, as the daggerlike leaves are indeed sharp.

CYCADS

Cycads, one of the oldest plant groups known, are actually primitive seed plants from the jungles of a former geological age. Morphologically they are the intermediate step in plant evolution from fern

Dizygotheca elegantissima (right) seems like a palm but it is really of the Aralia family.

Another palmlike plant is Cordyline, lush and green and easy to grow. (Hort Pix photo)

to flowering plant. The name Cycad is of Greek derivation and means palm; Cycads are often mistaken for palms because their appearance is very similar.

The plants are widely distributed and range from South America to New Guinea, the Fiji Islands, Australia, and Southern Africa.

Many Cycads look like tree ferns because of their stout trunks that are seldom branched, except in the genus Cycas. Their crowns of leaves resemble palm fronds and are leathery and smooth on the upper surface with scales on the under surface. The majority of Cycads are slow growing, and most are exceedingly decorative because of their sculptured form and graceful growth.

Hard to resist is *Dracaena marginata*, a member of the lily family with palmlike growth habit. (Molly Adams photo)

Cycads are impressive with their tapestry of leaves and always dramatic. (Jack Barnich photo)

This lovely plant is *Dion purpursii*, a member of the Cycad family. (Photo courtesy Architectural Pottery Company)

Plants require a shady place, although a few will adapt to a sunny location. The plants require liberal waterings and warmth, 60°F minimum at night. They appreciate some feeding when they start new growth, but only at that time and at no other time.

In this group of plants you will find a wealth of indoor beauty for little care and maintenance. Although the majority of Cycads are infrequently seen, occasionally you will find specimens at larger florists. I hope that in the future more growers will display them to the public. The better known genera of Cycads are Cycas, Macrozamia, Ceratozamia, Dion, and Zamia.

Ceratozamia mexicana. This Cycad grows to about 12 inches, with slightly flexible arching leaves and as many as 80 leaflets. The leaflets are 10- to 14-inches long and taper to a sharp point, lighter green underneath than on the surface.

C. purpusii. This plant has upright fronds with slender leaflets.

Cycas circinalis (fern palm). This is a stellar foliage plant, with arching stems and thin green leaves.

C. revoluta (sago palm). Here is probably one of the most ideal house plants you can grow. Leaves are dark green and shiny, to 30 inches long.

Dion edule. With palmlike leaves to 5 feet long and about 6 inches wide, *D. edule* makes a graceful house plant.

D. purpusi. This plant has a short trunk that grows to about 30 inches in length and erect stiff leaves. Makes an attractive house plant.

D. spinulosum. A slow-growing spiny plant that resembles a tree fern. Leaves grow in an elegant rosette pattern.

Macrozamia denisonii. A graceful ornamental plant with curving, feathery smooth fronds.

Zamia floridana. A small Cycad that looks like a dwarf palm, with 6-inch long leaflets.

7. Getting the Right Plant

Sometimes finding the right fern or palm for a particular place in the home requires more time than expected, because often you don't know how to locate a special plant. Usually you will want to deal with local sources—florists, nurseries. Some stock specimen plants; others do not. Visit the place (if possible) if it is a reasonable distance from your home. If such establishments are not in your region, mail-order houses that specialize in decorator plants are your best source.

Before you buy, study catalogs, read this book, and try to have some idea of what kind of fern or palm you need. Do you need a bushy rosette-type fern to complement the room design, or is a vertical plant like a fine palm what you want? As mentioned, ferns and palms are available in many different sizes and colors and are of many different growth habits. Each plant has a character, and even though any plant might do in a situation as a living green accent, the plant that "belongs" always gets a comment from guests.

LOCAL GARDEN CENTERS AND FLORISTS

Companies such as Terrestris (New York) and the Greenhouse (Chicago) specialize in large decorator plants. So do some florist shops and garden centers. These places are the prime source for a good plant and many times you can explain the growing conditions to the people there and they will recommend a likely plant.

However, if there is not a large supplier in your area, garden cen-

ters, patio shops, and plant nurseries are all sources of ferns or palms. The local florist may have some ferns or a few palms, but they may not be mature specimens. If your area is without a large nursery or florist, investigate mail-order houses.

Wholesale nurseries are another source of large plants, but you will have to deal through your local florist, who can order the plant for you. In this instance it is imperative you know exactly what you want (by name), how tall it should be, and so forth.

MAIL-ORDER SUPPLIERS

There are dozens of mail-order plant suppliers in the United States, and most advertise in garden magazines. Write for catalogs; if you do not see the fern or palm you want, send a letter asking for your specific plant. Do not be afraid to order large plants by mail. Air freight collect shipments (the cost is about $20 per hundredweight, which may seem excessive, but it isn't if you get exactly what you want) reach most places overnight and are a safe and dependable way of securing plants, although you must pick them up at the air-terminal freight office. Large plants purchased by mail order come in heavy cardboard boxes securely packed and usually reach you in perfect condition. When I lived in Chicago, most of my plants, which included large palms and Cycads to 8 feet tall, were brought in from Miami.

When you order, specify air freight collect and have the supplier put your phone number on the outside of the package, with instructions to call you immediately on arrival; then you are sure of getting your plants overnight. You can order plants practically all year, although remember that in winter severe weather can injure plants and in torrid summer weather heat can severely damage them.

Tell your supplier to leave the plants in their containers; this may not seem a wise economical move, but it is, because a mature plant uprooted from its container takes years to recover, if it recovers at all. Generally large plants are shipped in plastic containers, sometimes in large oil cans. Do not immediately repot the plants. If the

Fit the plant to the spot; here the bamboo palm (*Chamaedorea erumpens*) provides an interesting study in texture and leaf. (Photo by author)

Howea palms are at nurseries; come in many sizes. (Wilson photo)

appearance is unattractive (and it will be), slip the original container into an ornamental pot. After a few months, when the plant has adjusted to its new conditions, repot the plant.

THE PLANT FOR YOU

For ferns, many of which have long pendulous fronds, you need a pedestal, or suspend the plants in hanging baskets for dramatic effect. Many ferns like the Nephrolepis varieties and *Polypodium aureum* are natural basket plants as are some Davallias. Upright ferns for table accent include Adiantums and some Aspleniums. Platyceriums (stag's-horn ferns) are almost always grown on cork slabs, and for these you need wall space.

If you need a tall, vertical accent for a room corner or window wall, palms will no doubt be your first choice. However, just which palm to buy is important. Some, like the sentry palm *Howea forsteriana*, are graceful and tall with a spreading habit that is almost flamboyant. A palm like *Chamaedorea erumpens* is more vertical than spreading, and a palm like *Caroyota mitis* is really a sprawling plant, but it still has vertical overtones. The Chinese fan palm *Livistona chinensis* is graceful but spreading, and the scalloped leaves are especially handsome against white walls.

A list of mail-order suppliers follows. For local nurseries and garden centers see your phone book.

Alberts & Merkel Bros. Inc.
P.O. Box 537
Boynton Beach, Fla. 33435

Merry Gardens
Camden, Maine 04843

Roehrs Co.
P.O. Box 125
East Rutherford, N. J. 07073

8. The Many Decorative Uses of Ferns

Because of their elegant fronds, ferns are studies in form and design. Thus, they are not only interesting in their living state but they can be also fascinating when dried and placed in small frames; they make enchanting pictures or may be preserved for future viewing. Ferns are also attractive in terrariums—living gardens that can last for years; many ferns are dwarf by nature and thrive in a woodsy setting with small pieces of rock, etc. You might also want to use a column of greenery, that is, tiny ferns tucked into a sphagnum-covered wire tube. These are fascinating projects and provide unique decoration for the home.

FERNS IN PICTURES

No special skills or tools are required to dry fern fronds. However, mature fronds in excellent condition should be selected, and they should not have any moisture on them when going into the drying process. The drying methods are done by air drying (perhaps the easiest), pressing, or using a dehydrating medium such as silica gel, which is available as Flower Dri in packages at nurseries.

Do not allow fronds to shrivel; dry them immediately. Have the following materials ready so there will be no delay: newspapers, heavy books, rocks for weight, picture frame with glass, matteboard, scissors, and some household cement.

FERN CASE

Place fronds on the newspapers so they do not touch each other; newspaper will absorb the moisture squeezed from the fronds as they are pressed. (Heavy white blotting paper can also be used but it is expensive.) Use folded double sheets of newspapers and replace them every 2 or 3 days. Books can be set on top of the newspapers to aid in the pressing, but do not use heavy books; a weight sufficient to keep fronds from shifting but not too heavy to bruise them and cause a color predisposition is fine.

Fronds may also be dried and pressed in old books; since the materials may damage the pages be sure these are books you no longer care about. The paper must be absorbent; glossy pages will not work. Place a few rocks on the books to hold down the plant material.

When the fronds are dry mount them on matteboard or cardboard. The points of the fronds should be fastened with a little glue; work carefully because frequently dried fronds are particularly brittle.

Fern fronds to be pressed for pictures. (Hort Pix photo)

Fronds of Boston fern make handsome pictures. (Photo by author)

Humata
   tyermannii

Select a simple picture frame. A plain narrow frame generally looks best with fern fronds, which are usually small and delicate. With pressed-flower pictures the glass of the frame must come in direct contact with the plant material.

FERNS IN CASES

In Victorian times fern cases were immensely popular. These elegant pictures behind glass provide interest and fascination to all who see them (there are dozens of diminutive ferns that will prosper in a glass case). Cases can decorate any room when placed on a windowsill or table and last for years with little care.

The glass case can be a special unit or simply an aquarium with a glass top; a good size is 24 inches long, 16 inches wide, and about 20 inches high. The idea is to simulate a natural scene, using small rocks with charming ferns. In this terrarium condition tiny ferns thrive. The case provides an even temperature and ample humidity, and condensation running down the sides of the glass supplies moisture for the plants. In fact, you may not have to water for months.

To prepare the fernery, put in a 1-inch bed of pea gravel. On top of this scatter some charcoal granules to keep the soil sweet. Then prepare a 2- to 4-inch bed of rich, somewhat acid, soil for the plants. Select small rocks and stones and build up contours in the case. A flat expanse of soil is monotonous, so strive for hills and valleys where small ferns can be tucked into rock pockets. Install plants carefully, arranging them until a pleasing design is achieved. Once the case is completed, water the soil until it is uniformly damp and close the case. No more water will be required until the soil gets somewhat dry; then a gentle watering over the ground is all that is needed. Try to keep the foliage dry. If too much moisture condenses within the housing, remove the glass cover for a few hours a day.

Place taller-growing ferns in the back, toward the corners, and smaller plants in the front. Some mosses are extremely beautiful and can be used as ground covers to complement the ferns. Keep the fernery in a bright but not sunny location.

PLANTS FOR THE FERN CASE

Adiantum capillus-veneris (southern maidenhair fern)
A. cuneatum (delta maidenhair fern)

Woodwardia orientalis, the chain fern, has lovely sculptural fronds. (Photo by author)

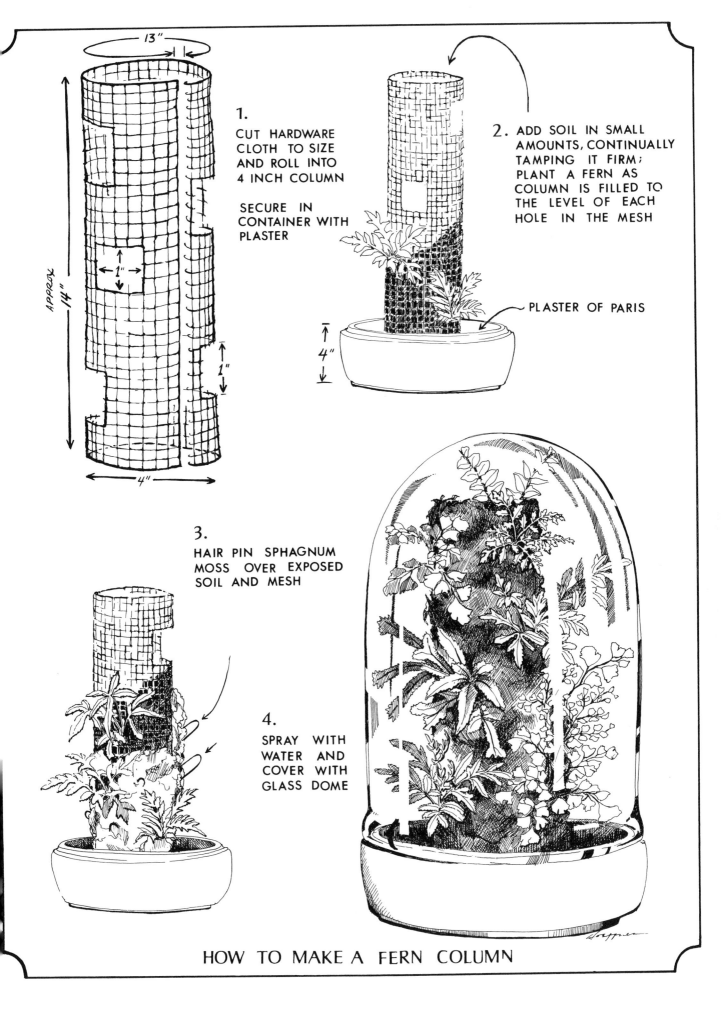

13"

1"

1"

APPROX. 14"

4"

1. CUT HARDWARE CLOTH TO SIZE AND ROLL INTO 4 INCH COLUMN

SECURE IN CONTAINER WITH PLASTER

2. ADD SOIL IN SMALL AMOUNTS, CONTINUALLY TAMPING IT FIRM; PLANT A FERN AS COLUMN IS FILLED TO THE LEVEL OF EACH HOLE IN THE MESH

PLASTER OF PARIS

4"

3. HAIR PIN SPHAGNUM MOSS OVER EXPOSED SOIL AND MESH

4. SPRAY WITH WATER AND COVER WITH GLASS DOME

HOW TO MAKE A FERN COLUMN

A. hispidulum (maidenhair fern)
Asplenium bulbiferum (mother fern)
A. trichomanes (maidenhair spleenwort)
Davallia mariesii
Humata tyermanni (bear's-foot fern)
Lygodium scandens
Microlepia strigosa
Pellaea rotundifolia (button fern)
Pteris cretica (brake fern)
P. ensiformis 'Victoriae'

Fern allies such as Selaginella species are also appropriate for the fern case.

FERN COLUMNS

This is an unusual but effective way of growing small ferns. The fern column is a wire mesh tube packed with osmunda or sphagnum in which the ferns are planted, the fronds coming through the wire as they grow. The wire mesh can be 12 to 16 inches tall when rolled into a tube; secure the tube with hooks or smaller wires. Then place the column in a dish or a flower pot and set it in place with a thin layer of cement to hold it upright.

Next tuck in sheet sphagnum moss or osmunda around the outside of the column; take your time and do it slowly so the moss adheres to the wires. Fill the column with a rich planting soil, tamping it down occasionally to make it firm.

Use small ferns inserted in the spaces between the wires of the column and sink them into place; if necessary secure them with thin-gauge galvanized wire. In a few months the ferns will climb the sphagnum and you will have a charming column of greenery. When the cylindrical garden is completed, mist it with water and cover it with a glass dome (these are available from suppliers.)

Young Davallia and Polypodium plants will grow lavishly on a fern column, as will small species of Pteris and Pelleae.

9. Plant Protection

You will find ferns and palms amazingly free of pests or disease, especially if you have mature specimens. Ferns and palms are just too tough for pests; their foliage is not as soft and inviting as that of other house plants.

Generally, if plants are not growing well and leaves are wan or stems soft, it is a question of poor culture, rarely crawling foes. Check growing conditions first before you suspect insects. If, however, you do see insects on your plants, there are several ways to eliminate them without resorting to poisonous chemicals, and by all means remember that most commercial pesticides will quickly kill a fern or palm rather than help it, for plants are highly susceptible to poisons.

OBSERVATION: THE KEY TO PREVENTION

Because generally your ferns and palms will be large and for decoration, and since you will probably grow only a few specimens, it is easy to watch for insects. As you wash foliage with a damp cloth, observe and catch insects before they have a chance to get a foothold.

Most of the common house-plant insects—aphids, scales, mealybugs, thrips—are recognizable on sight. Easy household remedies (discussed later) will do the job. If, however, you have been forgetful and a severe insect infestation occurs, there are ways of dealing with it.

This fern has been poorly grown and lacks good symmetry; it has further been abused by being placed against a wall.

When you buy your plants, make a thorough inspection of foliage and stems. There is absolutely nothing wrong in scrutinizing a plant for insects; in greenhouses with other plants they are more prone to insect attack than they would be in the home. This is the time to find the culprits, not later when they are installed at home. If possible, soak new plants to the rim of the pot in a tub of water (the bathtub is fine) for several hours. You will be surprised at the unwelcome guests that may come to the surface, because often soil harbors insidious insects.

MEANS OF PROTECTION

Keeping leaves clean and hosing down foliage are the best ways of having troublefree plants. Do this early in the morning so all foliage is dry by evening. A strong hose spray flushes out any bug that might be hiding in folded leaves and is one of the best preventives against insects.

Mealybugs occasionally attack plants but can be eradicated with cotton swabs dipped in alcohol. (USDA photo)

Since your plants will be in the home, it may be difficult to move them to an area to hose them down thoroughly. In this case, use one of the spray bottles available at nurseries. Fill it with water and syringe plants generously on warm days. In winter, limit the washing to once every six weeks, for lingering moisture on leaves and cloudy days can cause fungus disease.

If insects do attack a plant, use a soap and water solution (not a detergent). Half a bar of Fels Naptha or laundry soap mixed with 4 quarts of water is fine. Repeat the washing several times during the week, and flush residue from the plant with clear lukewarm water. Aphids, mealybugs, and thrips will respond to the laundry soap-and-water treatment.

Aphids are green, black, or yellow oval-shaped demons only ⅛ inch long. They are especially troublesome among house plants and may attack ferns and palms too if they are in the same area. To control, use soapy water solution, Black Flag 40, or swab insects with a cotton swab dipped in alcohol.

Scale are parasites and appear as brown protuberances on the plant. Their shell-like covering makes it difficult to kill them, but they can cause serious damage or even destroy a plant if they get out of control. They prefer leathery leaves like the Cyrtomiums and Pellaeas. Control them by using a cotton swab dipped in alcohol or Black Flag 40 solution (Do not confuse scale insects with seed spores that form on fertile fronds.)

Mealybugs are white, easy to see, and form dense colonies in leaf axils and along plant stalks. They multiply quickly, so get rid of them immediately. Use a solution of soapy water applied at three-day intervals for two weeks.

Thrips are small insects only about 1/16 inch long, white when young and black when mature. They feed on the outer coatings of leaves and, once marked, foliage remains blemished. Use mild applications of Black Flag 40 solution spaced three days apart for two weeks.

Slugs and snails occasionally will attack indoor plants; they are easily recognizable. They can be controlled with a few grains of bran scattered near the container. Slugs and snails do their work at night, so gather them from the bran and destroy them in the morning.

Ants can cause a plague among ferns and palms because they har-

Red spider is an occasional pest of ferns. (USDA photo)

bor various insects (aphids and scales) and herd them into plantations where they derive nourishment from the exudation of the insects. There are many household remedies for ants, depending on your part of the country. If you are averse to using poisons in the home, use a piece of thick rope about 12 inches long dipped in syrup and coated with sugar. The ants will go to these strips, which from time to time can be removed and dipped into boiling water.

GROOMING PLANTS

Your ferns and palms are always on display, so be sure they are perfectly groomed and trained. Cut off dead or decayed fronds and trim brittle leaf edges (use small sterile manicure scissors). After trimming stalks or stems, dust the cut portions with powdered charcoal to thwart fungus from developing.

Turn plants occasionally so all parts of the foliage are exposed to light. This is especially important with ferns. Lopsided plants are rarely attractive; you want plants that are symmetrically pleasing in all aspects.

Do not use leaf-shining solutions on foliage because they do more harm than good: they clog the pores of the leaves and can lead to loss of foliage. Do, however, wash palm leaves frequently, and hose down fern foliage as previously mentioned.

With ferns in optimum conditions, adventitious aerial roots form. These are of no value and do nothing but sap strength from a growing plant. Cut away all aerial roots when you see them.

10. Starting Your Own Plants

Many gardeners are interested in propagating their own plants because they enjoy the economy and the satisfaction of growing seedlings into mature beauties. It costs nothing to get more plants, and in a few years these small plants become ideal subjects for table and window accent.

Ferns produce spores, not seeds, on the underside of leaves. (The spores look like small brown dots.) The most popular and sure way to get new ferns from old ones is to grow them from the tiny and brown seedlike attachments. This is not an exact or time-consuming process, but it does take some experience and tact to succeed. However, it offers great adventure, and seeing the development from spore to fern is fascinating. If you are less industrious you might want to try some of the easier ways of increasing plants: by division of crowns or by rooting adventitious growths found on the surface of certain fronds. Either method is ridiculously simple and almost foolproof. Futhermore, trimming the crowns aids the plant, for it prevents the drain of nutrients and makes the fern more attractive.

FROM SPORES

There are various methods and means of growing ferns from spores, but the basic process is the same. Cut fertile fronds (those with brown dots on the back) from plants, and put them with the spore side down on a piece of paper or cardboard (gathering the spores at the proper time means taking them when they start to turn brown). Allow the leaves to remain on the paper for a few days. Tap the fronds gently to remove the spores. Spores can then be guided into a small bottle and capped with the name of the species, but it is best to sow the spores as soon as possible. Although ferns may be sown at any time of the year, spring offers the most favorable months, for then they have sufficient time to develop crowns strong enough to withstand dark and gray winter days.

There are several ways to germinate spores, but I use shallow azalea pans and a sphagnum-and-humus-and-sand medium (use sterilized soil.) Dust the spores lightly on the surface of the medium; do not cover them. Bottom-water pans for a few hours and set them into glass terrariums with a top. If too much condensation forms, remove the top a few hours a day. Until the spores have formed little crowns, water by partially immersing the container, allowing the lower part of the pan to stand in water until sufficient moisture is absorbed.

Place the pans in the cases in a shady but not dark corner. Spores differ in germinating time: some start growing within a few days, others take weeks. In a few months start watering the pans with a light mist, rather than by immersion. When you see the first flush of green on the surface of the medium you are looking at the beginning ferns (they do not look like plants). They are called prothalli; this green fuzz is a one-celled body with rootlike hairs that fasten into soil. One cell after another develops until there is a heart-shaped formation about ¼ inch in size. From this the new fern sprouts. When seedlings are evident and start to crowd each other, thin them so the remaining ones have room to develop. At this point remove the azalea pan from its protective case and start growing the ferns in a permanent window location. By the end of the first year seedlings will be ready for individual pots.

Damping off is a fungus that frequently affects young ferns, so take steps to prevent this disease. Warmth and moisture help accelerate fungi growth; if you see grayish mold forming on new plants use a damping-off powder (available at nurseries) according to directions on the package.

BY DIVISION

Besides starting ferns from spores, you might want to reproduce them by division of crowns, since this is really a simple method that can be done at repotting time. Some ferns naturally form several

cut

cut

rootstock

FERN PROPAGATION BY DIVISION

crowns and can be notched with a sterile knife, and each crown should be taken with a set of roots (wait until plants show two distinct crowns before cutting one off). Do not completely cut the plant from its neighbor; simply make a V cut and then pull apart gently with your hands. The best time for division is in spring when warm weather approaches, enabling plants to make satisfactory growth. Place the new plant in soil in a small container (do not use a large one as soil will turn sour), and for a few weeks keep it under surveillance. Keep soil moderately moist and temperatures as constant as possible.

Ferns that have creeping rhizomes, such as Polypodiums, Davallias, and others, may be propagated freely by cutting and potting sections of the rhizomes. Put the rhizomes in a light, well-drained, porous soil mix but do not bury them; just give them a superficial covering of the medium, and place pans or pots in a warm and humid but not sunny location. In a short time small green specks should be evident and new plants on the way.

OTHER MEANS OF PROPAGATION

Ferns can also be propagated from buds or bulblets that appear on mature plants. These minute plantlets are seen on *Asplenium bulbiferum* and some Woodwardia species. Bulblets develop on the frond; these may be anchored in sandy leaf mold until roots form. Then the individual small plants may be separated from the frond and potted. Provide sufficient heat (78°F) and humidity so they can prosper.

Still another way of getting new plants from old ones is to take the tops of trunks of some tree ferns—Cibotiums especially—and *Alsophila australis*. Cut about 6 to 8 inches from the top of the trunk; place it in a container with gravel and water and when roots form put the plantlet in a new pot with soil. Or you can grow it on in the same container.

PALMS

Palms are propagated by seeds or by division or from offshoots. For the amateur gardener the latter is the easiest and most practical way of getting new plants. This process involves taking the small plant that develops at the base of the mother plant and growing it on. It is a simple procedure, for the offshoots or suckers already have

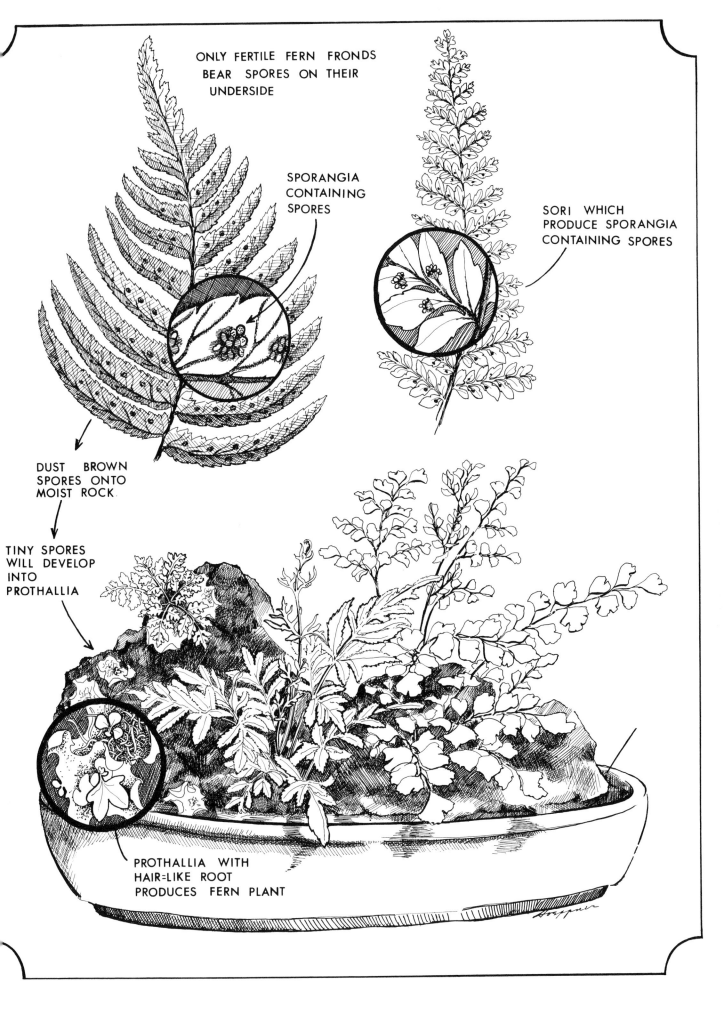

ONLY FERTILE FERN FRONDS
BEAR SPORES ON THEIR
UNDERSIDE

SPORANGIA
CONTAINING
SPORES

SORI WHICH
PRODUCE SPORANGIA
CONTAINING SPORES

DUST BROWN
SPORES ONTO
MOIST ROCK.

TINY SPORES
WILL DEVELOP
INTO
PROTHALLIA

PROTHALLIA WITH
HAIR=LIKE ROOT
PRODUCES FERN PLANT

leaves and root systems. Cut them from the mature plant when they are about 6 to 10 inches high and pot them in a good porous soil. Do this in spring when warm weather will encourage healthy growth.

Chamaerops, Rhapis, Phoenix, Chamaedoreas, and other clump or cluster palms can be divided. This is best done at repotting time in spring. Divide crowns with a sterile knife (run a match flame over blade) and pot divisions in porous soil in 5- or 6-inch containers. Keep soil evenly moist.

Glossary of Terms

adventitious growth—a growth in plants that appears in an unusual place or in an irregular or sporadic manner

aerial roots—roots borne in the air rather than underground or under water

aphids—small insects that suck the juices of plants

bone meal—crushed or ground bone used as a feed or fertilizer for plants

buds, bulblets—a lateral or terminal protuberance growth on the stem of a plant; an undeveloped shoot

damping off—a plant disease caused by fungus in the soil

epiphytic plants—ferns that grow on other plants upon which they depend for mechanical support but not as a source of nourishment

fern-allies—plants that resemble ferns

fertile fronds—fronds that bear spores

friable soil—brittle, readily crumbled soil

fronds—the foliage of ferns

humus—a brown or black substance formed in the last stages of the decomposition of animal or vegetable matter leaching—a method of removing excess salts or other impurities from soil by water

leaf axils—the angle between the upper surface of a leaf stalk and the stem from which it arises

leaf mold—humus or compost consisting of decomposed leaves and other organic material

loam—soil consisting mainly of sand, clay, silt, and organic matter

mealybug—an insect that feeds on plants; identifiable by the white powdery substance that covers it

nomenclature—systematic naming of plants

offshoots—lateral shoots from the main stem of a plant

osmunda—fibrous roots used as a potting medium for cultivated plants

palmate formation—having leaflets or lobes radiating or diverging from one point, as a palmate leaf

peat moss—partly carbonized remains of sphagnum moss, used as a mulch and plant food

petioles—the stalk by which a leaf is attached to a stem

pinnate foliage—having leaflets, lobes, or divisions in a featherlike arrangement on each side of a common axis

prothallus—a small, flat mass of tissue produced by a germinating spore of ferns, bearing sexual organs and developing into a mature plant

rhizomes—a thickened underground stem that spreads by creeping

rosette—a small cluster of leaves arranged in a circular overlapping pattern, similar to rose petals

scale—sucking insects injurious to plants

shards—pieces of broken pottery used in the bottom of containers to provide good drainage

silica gel—a dehydrating medium used to dry ferns

sori—clusters of spore cases borne on the undersides of fronds

species—member of a genus
sphagnum moss—a group of mosses native to bogs
spores—reproductive cells that are capable of producing new plants
sterile fronds—fronds that don't bear spores

top-dressing—replacing top 3 to 4 inches of old soil with fresh soil

variety—a subspecies